Seven Questions Jesus Asked

Seven Questions Jesus Asked

R. BENJAMIN GARRISON

ABINGDON PRESS

NASHVILLE   NEW YORK

SEVEN QUESTIONS JESUS ASKED

Copyright © 1975 by Abingdon Press

Library of Congress Cataloging in Publication Data

GARRISON, R. BENJAMIN. Seven questions Jesus asked.
Includes bibliographical references.
1. Jesus Christ—Words—Meditations. I. Title
BT306.G33   232.9'54   74-19266

ISBN 0-687-38194-0

MANUFACTURED BY THE PARTHENON PRESS AT
NASHVILLE, TENNESSEE, UNITED STATES OF AMERICA

CONTENTS

TO

JOSEPH N. PEACOCK

Colleague in ministry
for more than a dozen years
Authentic Christian
Friend

PREFACE

The discovery of truth depends almost as much upon the adequacy of one's questions as upon the accuracy of one's answers. Education has long understood this. Religion is beginning to. If you are watching a basketball game and your seat partner asks, "Do you think they'll make a touchdown?" it hardly covers the case to answer, "No." If you ask an inaccurate question, even the right answer is wrong.

This emphasis upon the importance of questions is known in philosophy as the "Socratic method." Socrates considered himself the intellectual midwife of Athens. He went about asking probing, stinging questions designed to help the answerer understand that he, the student, had brought the conclusions out of himself and that they were, therefore, more acceptable. If under this kind of cross-questioning a person came to feel that he really did not know much, he would begin to ask questions more seriously and more carefully.

Bulletin Cover 3/5/82

Jesus was a master question-asker: "Who do men say that I am?" He was also a wise question-answerer: "Go, take up thy cross, and follow me." But sometimes he refused to answer a question. He seems to have known from the start of his ministry what some of us never learn, namely, that it is futile to talk to people in their own terms if those terms themselves are wrong. There were, no doubt, a variety of reasons why he occasionally refused to answer a question: sometimes the questioner was not sincere; sometimes it was framed in the wrong terms; sometimes it was simply unanswerable.

For more than a decade I have been fascinated by the question-category in the ministry of Jesus: the questions he answered, the questions he posed, the questions he parried.

What we quickly discover is that, however he disposed of a specific question, he always dealt with the questioner seriously. Out of seemingly inexhaustible resources of insight, intuition, and sensitivity he knew his man or woman, their needs, fears, and yearnings. The result was that beneath the language, whether theirs or his, a personal meeting was transacted and often a personal transformation was born. He was, so to say, a kind of Jewish Socrates who "knew what goes on in their hearts" (John 2:25, *Today's English Version*) and who labored, with kindness and with candor, to introduce persons to the truth about themselves. —R. Benjamin Garrison, Seven Questions

In this book I present some of the fruit of these *new, cultural.*

interrogatory reflections, focusing especially upon seven of the questions Jesus asked.

In doing so I have been aided, once more, by my Christian community, the Wesley United Methodist Church and Foundation of Urbana, Illinois. Herein, with them, I have experienced what I am convinced is the freest pulpit-pew in the Church. I put it so (pulpit-pew) because the one requires the other. There is no such thing as a free pulpit without a responsible and responsive pew, and vice versa. Furthermore, much of what follows in this book has been enabled because, for many years, the "pew" part of this equation has afforded the "pulpit" part a generous annual study leave for research, reflection, and writing. For that, and for them, I continue to be inexpressibly grateful.

It is customary, and I have always been glad to follow that custom, to thank one's secretary. In the case of this book, however, I am not only glad but obliged to do so. It was the publisher, rather than the author, who produced date and deadline complications. Had it not been for Louise Gish, secretary extraordinary and friend undeserved, this project would not and could not have come to birth. Once more, as with earlier books, I am in debt to her beyond repaying.

I have dedicated this effort to my friend and colleague of more than a dozen years, Joseph N. Peacock. Over the frantic and sometimes frightening decade of the sixties, and now into the quieter but no less crucial seventies, we have labored together in common ministry—studying, arguing, planning, praying, trusting, confessing, and celebrating. It is rare for two ministers to have that many years together in one place, at one task, with one purpose. Joe has contributed so much to the result, and with such unbudgeable integrity, that it is a joy and a privilege to say this affectionate "thanks."

R. BENJAMIN GARRISON

Chapter I

THE QUESTION OF SENSITIVITY
"Who Touched Me?"
(MARK 5:31)

In *Camelot* the authors, Lerner and Lowe, set the subject up for us: sensitivity. We are going to think in this chapter about the question of sensitivity. *Camelot* deals in part with that question. At times the play deals with it explicitly. First we have Lancelot, the incredibly good young knight (I mean that quite literally: his goodness is unbelievable). He leaves the impression that he was starched before he was washed. He gives goodness such a bad name that the whole company finally cries out, in a burst of defiance and relief, "Fie on Goodness, Fie!" Lancelot is *in*sensitive to the vibrations he sends out to other people and is insensitive to their answering resentments.

Then there is that tortured and poignant scene wherein Lancelot comes to Guinevere's room, declares his sincere but illicit love for the wife of his friend King Arthur. Guinevere—confused, ambivalent, torn by a torrent of colliding desires—spurns his entreaties and advances. Lancelot cries of the torture he is in, oblivious to the torture she is in. It is at this point in the play that Guinevere makes the sensitivity point for us. She shouts to Lancelot, "Oh! the insensitivity of sensitive men!" There is an irony in that which, one guesses, Guinevere herself misses. She is right about Lancelot but seems to miss the fact that *she* is being insensitive to him at the same time. That is not so very strange because most of us are rather better at picking out the failures of other folks than we are at staring squarely at our own.

But quite apart from the irony, she is also rather wrong. For at that moment Lancelot is not so much being sensitive as he is being selfish, at least in the positive sense of the word I intend in this chapter in raising the question of sensitivity.

I

The biblical setting for our inquiry has been long neglected and is therefore not a very familiar one. Jesus is on a quite important journey to attend to a grievously ill and possibly dead young girl. Further he has been besought by the girl's father who is one of the "rulers of the synagogue," the chairman of the Administrative Board, or the Clerk of the Session, as it were. En route Jesus is thronged and pressed by a great crowd who are seeking him out because they have heard of this great preacher-teacher-healer from Nazareth. In the crowd is a woman with a severe gynecological problem: she has been bleeding constantly for twelve years! Later we shall see what she had tried to do about her malady. For the moment I note only that she believed that this fabled figure named Jesus could heal her, even if the contact between the two of them consisted merely of her touching the hem of his garment. So she touched him, gently, tentatively, fearfully. Right then, according to the story, her bleeding ceased. Jesus simultaneously felt or sensed that something, some strength, had gone out of him. Immediately he asked, "Who touched me?" His disciples were astonished. Here was this great throng, yet he wanted to know what one person had touched him! It was as if a pitcher at Yankee Stadium should ask what individual in the stands of shouting fans had called his name. The woman had not expected to be detected. But, having been, she tells Jesus what had happened. And he sends her forth with infinite tenderness, "Daughter, . . . go in peace" (Mark 5:34).

II

In order to recapture even a little of the shock and drama that this event megaphoned across the countryside, let us imagine a little. Imagine a modern medical doctor, say a literary type like Dr. Spock or Fritz Kunkel, publicizing a medical record even remotely like what three of the Gospels have preserved here. Suppose Dr. Somebody were to write and print the following: "Ms. X. Y. She has been afflicted since 1963 with Somethingorotheritis. During that time she has spent every cent she has earned on physicians' fees, X rays, and miracle drugs." (Every cent she has earned! Talk about the spiraling, skyrocketing of medical costs!) "Now, in 1975, twelve years later, we are obliged to report that she has not been cured. Not only that, but competent medical opinion indicates that, despite the $17,469.18 she has expended, her physical condition is worse on January 15, 1975, than it was on January 15, 1963." Whatever else you might give that physician, he should certainly get an "A" for honesty.

Maybe this is the reason that Luke, who was a physician himself, toned down his version a tad. He told the truth, but not the whole truth, leaving out that damning and damaging phrase, "But rather [she] grew worse." (Mark 5:26b). No indeed: one thing we can be clear about, for once, is that this medical record (whether it was characterized by ineptitude, frustration, or both) was not recorded and preserved by the Galilean Medical Association. The woman was, frankly, an embarrassment and a judgment.

With that as historical background I turn now to some consideration of what we can learn from this story.

We learn first that *sensitivity is a discerning experience.* Jesus manifested it, showed it, shared it with one person who could easily have been lost, and usually would have been lost, in the crowd. Here were numberless people pressing upon him, thronging him, pushing and touching him; yet out of that mass he was aware of *one*: one person, one need, one touch. I remember standing along a parade route one day in Panama City. It was their "Fourth of July," albeit on November 3, marking the Panamanian independence from Columbia in 1903. One could scarcely move for the crush; one could hardly hear for the cries of several hundreds of thousands of people. Then I became aware of a slight, and slightly different, pressure on my leg. I looked down to see two big brown eyes set in a small black face, wordlessly begging me to help him see the passing pageantry and color. So I hoisted him, smiling, onto my shoulders. In that throng and press it was nothing short of incredible that I should have sensed him near. I relate this merely to suggest, by rough analogy, how very precious was the fact that Jesus sensed and finally saw this single, lonely, seeking woman in that insistent crowd. His sensitivity was a discerning experience.

It was *also a generous one*. Notice how he placed the most gracious possible construction upon her deed. Of course an element of superstition subsisted beneath her belief that, if she could touch the fringe of his garment (Luke 8:44), she would, somehow, find healing and wholeness. In her desperation she was a little like the mariners in the opening scene of *The Tempest*, the shipwreck scene, when they cried,

All lost! to prayers, to prayers! all lost!

This woman was like that. Yet Jesus did not chide her for her superstition or attempt to update her theology (though that is, sometimes, a perfectly legitimate enterprise). Rather what he did was give her act the most gracious possible reception, saying simply, "Your faith has made you well" (Mark 5:34). Sensitivity, for him, was generosity.

Further, *it was a draining experience.* Surely anyone in the helping vocations will understand what I mean by that. One simply cannot enter empathetically and sympathetically into the agony of another without giving some vitality from one's very self. It is a demanding, almost a debilitating, experience. During the summer I sometimes spend long hours felling trees, cutting them up, cording them in the barn or basement. But the expenditure of energy involved in this physical labor is as nothing alongside the emotional exhaustion involved in counseling a suffering human being. Sensitivity is a draining experience, so much so that we can understand what was meant when the Gospel writers recorded, after this event, "Jesus felt that power had gone out of him" (Mark 5:30, *Today's English Version*).

Once more, for Jesus *sensitivity was an endearing experience.* He called the woman "Daughter," though she was probably not far from his own age. Having felt her anguish, her need, and her faith, he (as we too easily say) identified with her. Two human beings were, at that moment, in touch. A contact had been established. A relationship had begun. This one person was no longer just *any* one but a special person. A nobody became somebody: "Daughter."

III

What, then, is sensitivity?

At the minimum, it involves being in touch with yourself. The authors of a rather romanticized, but nevertheless interesting, book called *Please Touch* put it this way:

> Touching is wonder.
>   We think of it as reaching *out*
>   to know
>   to grow
>   to explore
>   to love
>   to believe.
> But there is also reaching
>   *within* . . .
> an inside touching that comes first. [1]

Indeed, unless that "inside touching" does come first we may not realistically entertain much hope of creative contact with others.

I heard this illustrated one winter night in a New Jersey living room. The fascinating young man who did most of the talking is in several ways a neurotic. But (and I say this quite seriously) he is a very creative neurotic. He has begun to understand what he is angry about. He is in touch with himself. If he were not, I very much doubt that we could or would have

[1] Edwin M. McMahon and Peter A. Campbell, *Please Touch* (New York: Sheed & Ward, 1969).

had the engaging evening of conversation that we mutually enjoyed.

However, this truth, that one must be in touch with oneself in order to be sensitive to others, has a soft underbelly, a darker and less pleasant side. The plain fact is that usually both sensitivities are simultaneously required. That is, in order to feel the hurts and hopes of others you must be temperamentally equipped to feel them in your own insides. The boast that you are able to let personal criticism roll off you like water off a duck's back is appropriate only if you are a duck. If you really can sit that loosely to what most other people would be distressed by, or maybe even destroyed by, then you probably do not care, or notice, what happens to other people either.

Similarly, it is also difficult to be "in touch" with God unless you are in touch with yourself. I should not want to sum this up psychologically or make an absolute or it, but I am increasingly convinced that there is a direct relationship between the capacity to believe in God and the ability to believe in yourself. Self-doubt seldom renders religious faith. Belief is of a piece. The sundering of it at one point weakens it otherwhere.

IV

Finally, I propose to look at the question, What does sensitivity require or entail?

Consider, for one thing, a sense of timing. How

important that is, and in how many areas of life! It is almost axiomatic that timing characterizes the good comedian, Jack Benny being perhaps the classic contemporary case. Timing also marks the effective liturgist, capable of carrying a congregation along on the wings of words and actions that move or pause or climb or kneel according to the many moods and postures of the soul. Wars are won or lost by timing. Marriages are undertaken or undermined because somebody has the good sense to ask or the bad sense to argue at precisely the right—or the wrong—time. Timing is a timely matter in all of life.

Not least in the sensitive life. Jesus, as we have seen, was on an urgent mission when this incident occurred. Yet because he was sensitive to the right time, it became far from incidental. How often the "word spoken in due season" (Proverbs 15:23 KJV) is remembered, with lasting influence, whereas the word too late, or the word another is not ready for, is wasted. Sensitivity requires an inner clock that measures the spirit's readiness with precision and with care.

Sensitivity also recognizes the evident but often overlooked fact that we live in a world made up of other persons. "No man is an island" was Donne's by now almost commonplace way of putting it. No one becomes a person alone. George Herbert Meade taught us this psychological fact many years ago. Paul taught us the parallel theological fact many years before. "We are members one of another." (Ephesians

4:25) That means that when you hurt, I do, or ought to. That means that I become what I become, and you do too, very largely out of the complex of ties and tenderness, of hurts and harshness, that bind us together and make us one.

Or, to revert to what we observed at the outset, sensitivity requires seeing the one among the many. At some point we must, we really must, gain the capacity to read statistics with compassion: to feel the problem of world hunger in terms of the growling belly and tearful eyes of an identified child whose name you know; to judge the abortion question in terms of a known couple's anguish; to feel fear with a fearful friend, and hope with her too, no matter how many fearless people she may be compared with or surrounded by.

Sensitivity, as Jesus demonstrated, requires placing the most generous possible construction upon another's words or deeds. That is tough sometimes. Recently when I found myself mildly irritated at the almost semi-weekly letter of one of my most persistent critics, I found it helpful to remind myself that, this time, out of five things he had commented upon, I had (in his judgment) struck out on only three. Sensitivity, as an old song reminds us, requires us to "accentuate the positive."

Again, as with Jesus' healing the woman, sensitivity demands the willingness to be drained. There is no way (at least I have discovered no way) to suffer with another's sorrows except to suffer; no way to exult in another's joy except to give out joy. Sympathy, says one, is your pain in my heart (or my pain in yours), and there is no costless way for that to happen.

Lastly, as in this woman's experience with Jesus, your sensitivity should be an endearing experience, literally: an experience that makes another dear to you. Jesus called this unnamed woman "Daughter," which meant, I am sure, that he had much rather suffer in her stead if he could; that her well-being was at least as important as his own; that even had she resisted or rejected him, he still would have sought and sheltered, healed and helped. In short, the two had become "dear" to each other.

> A famous Japanese sculptor
> once confounded the curators
> of an American art gallery
> where his works were being shown.
>
> At the base of each statue
> the sculptor had placed
> a polite little sign.
>
> The signs all read:
>
> "PLEASE TOUCH."[2]

So John Greenleaf Whittier's hymn "Our Master":

> We touch him in life's throng and press,
> And we are whole again.

[2] *Ibid.*

Chapter II

THE QUESTION OF BROTHERHOOD
"Who Are My Brothers?"
(MATTHEW 12:46-50)

In his Beecher lectures Bishop Gerald Kennedy relates a story about an old man, walking down the street one day and seeing a small boy minding a baby. "Son," he asked, "what is your little brother's name?" The lad glanced up and replied, "If he was my brother his name might be Jack, but he ain't and her name is Ruth."[1] Inevitably the man got the wrong answer.

Jesus, like many of the wise persons of all the ages, understood that one will nearly always get the wrong answer if one asks the wrong question. Much earlier Socrates had demonstrated that humans know more than they have realized until someone is astute enough to ask the right, revealing questions. In our own century the Soviet geneticist Lysenko asked in effect the thinly disguised question, "What kind of

[1] Gerald Kennedy, *God's Good News* (New York: Harper, 1955), p. 17.

gene is consistent with communist materialist philosophy?'' and thus later came to the astonishing (and false) conclusion that wheat could produce rye. Inept questions almost inevitably produce inexact answers.

This book is based upon the affirmation that Jesus' answers to life's questions deserve to be taken seriously because he asked the right questions.

This chapter's question is, Who are my brothers?

I

Three of the four Gospels record the event, although Mark provides an interestingly different interpretation as to why Mary and her younger sons sought Jesus out. It was, says Mark, because they had heard a report that Jesus was ''beside himself'' (3:21) or, as several modern translators render it, that he was ''out of his mind.''[2] This was probably not the first and surely not the last time that Jesus or his followers would be thought a little crazy. Nevertheless, we need not read any harsh or heartless or even unsympathetic motives into this family visitation. If they honestly believed, or thought others believed, that he was emotionally disturbed, it would have been natural for them to want to shelter and protect him.

Anyway, for whatever reasons they sought him out, someone said to Jesus:

[2] New English Bible, the Riverside New Testament, Moffatt, Weymouth, and the Jerusalem Bible, among others.

"Look, your mother and your brother are over there wanting to talk to you." But he replied to the man who told him this, "Who is a mother to me, and who are brothers?" And, pointing to his disciples, he said, "Behold these men are my mother and my brothers! For anyone who obeys the will of my heavenly Father, that person is my brother and sister and mother." (Matthew 12:47b-50)[3]

Before proceeding to a more detailed examination of this passage, note an interesting linguistic fact about this passage, a fact that, before I commenced to write this chapter, I had not noticed. A great deal of understandable and legitimate concern is being expressed nowadays about unnecessary and sometimes oppressive sexist language in our literature, including our religious literature. For example, the almost exclusive reference to deity as "he" rather than the more inclusive, and equally biblical, "God is spirit" (John 4:24a). For another example, the increasing sensitivity to the fact that otherwise beautiful hymns like Whittier's "O brother man, fold to thy heart thy brother" can leave the cumulative impression that Christian sisters don't count or don't exist. Note, though, the creative and freeing interplay between the words in this passage. Jesus asks, "Who is my brother?" Then, by way of answering his own question, he stretches forth his hand toward his disciples—twelve men—and says,

[3] In this chapter, as in a few other places in this volume, I have attempted to refurbish my rather bedraggled grasp of the Greek text by preparing, with the help of others, my own translation. Unless otherwise designated, therefore, references to Matthew 12 are from this source.

"These—these men—are my mother—and my brothers—and my sisters." In asking the question of brotherhood, Jesus was asking after and inviting us toward a universal relationship, a category that transcends gender or class or nation. "For anyone who obeys the will of my heavenly Father, that person is my brother and sister and mother." "There is neither Jew nor Greek, there is neither slave nor free, there is neither male nor female; for you are all one in Christ Jesus" (Galatians 3:28). The question of brotherhood is simultaneously the question of sisterhood.

II

Not that we should infer from this (or from anything else in Jesus' life, for that matter) that the Master was contemptuous of family ties or of filial affection. Perhaps he knew the proverb of his people, "There are no praises and no blessings for those who are ashamed of their families." Anyway, he acted as if he knew that truth. He was exhibiting here a healthy tension between the claims of his clan and the claims of his Creator. These claims may be, perhaps often, commensurate with each other. But they can collide. If they do, and when they do, the higher loyalty is the heavenly one.

Indeed I would insist that it was precisely because Jesus took the domestic ties with such high seriousness that he felt obediently obliged to challenge and qualify them. It is no great task and no great feat to question or resist the authority of a family whom one does not really respect. The shoe does begin to pinch, however—really pinch—when wearing it requires you to use that shoe to walk away from what your family stands for.

Really, it is the old story, the story of idolatry. Luther suggests somewhere that children are to obey the commandment to honor their parents except where to obey would be to break the first commandment: "Thou shalt have no other gods before me" (Deuteronomy 5:7, American Standard Version), not even parents, not even godly parents. The authority of family may not be permitted to escalate into authoritarianism. Its value is penultimate, not final.

That is, for Jesus as for any ethically sensitive follower of his, "one of life's hardest battles [is] not . . . against hate but . . . against love."[4] "Smother love" is harder to combat than is overt hatred. The tender trap is finally the fiercest adversary of all. Jerome, writing in the fourth century, spoke tellingly of "the battering ram of natural affection" That is a devastating and terribly descriptive metaphor. That very tender thing, natural affection, which could and should urge, invite, and engender, can instead repress, condemn, and destroy. While giving full value to what familial affection can be, Jesus is suggesting that that value is never adequate, never ultimate, never enough.

If we see this, we may give full weight to what these

[4] *The Interpreter's Bible* (New York and Nashville: Abingdon-Cokesbury Press, 1951), VII, 695a.

things meant to Jesus: kith and kin, hearth and home. Surely he would not have chosen and transformed the word "Father" as his best name for God had it not pointed a depth and a light which elaborated his love and illuminated his life. Just because "mother" and "father" meant so much, he knew more surely "how subtly and powerfully love of family can sometimes compete with loyalty to the Kingdom of God" (*Interpreter's Bible*, VIII, 153b). The good *is* sometimes the enemy of the best: its competition, its substitute, its deputy—and its destroyer.

Consider: in religion we too easily settle for the penultimate—for the feeling that eases, or the pain that agonizes but not for the truth that illuminates and frees; in ethics we too easily settle for the helpful maxim rather than for the demanding duty; in domestic life we too easily settle for the comfortable routine rather than for the vulnerable opportunity; in politics we too easily settle for the expedient explanation instead of the costly alternative. Who was it who said that the saddest thought in the world is the thought of what might have been? What makes it sad, however, is the way we reject it; the prophets or preachers, the parents or teachers, the pains or purposes, the leaders or lessons that could, if we would let them, bring these truths home to our hearts.

III

Jesus, then, describes succinctly who my brother/sister/father/mother is—who my spiritual family is: "anyone who obeys the will of my heavenly Father."

Anyone? Surely not! Surely so! He may bear a strange name or wear a strange garb or kneel at a strange altar, or, observably, at no altar at all. She may be working for some things you do not care about or in some ways you cannot approve. They may have some habits or follow some customs or hallow some beliefs that seem to you alien or absurd. He or she or they may live next door or across the world. Still it stands: "*Anyone* who obeys the will of my heavenly Father, that person is my brother and sister and mother."

Anyone. How exquisitely and distressingly universal. Color does not count, nor nation nor class; creeds cannot cut you off, not legitimately. Intelligence does not weigh for brotherhood or against sisterhood except as it is or is not used as an instrument for God's plan and purpose. How we feel is subordinate to how we place our feelings at the disposal of the divine. *Anyone* who does the will—period.

That has a cosmic sweep to it that hushes what is parochial, hallows what is universal, and harbingers a new age and a new humanity. Whatever silly little lines we try to draw in order to divide it are bound at the last to be erased. Whatever artificial barriers we erect to restrict it are sure in the end to fall. Brotherhood, sisterhood, familyhood is the destiny of us all. We may delay it, but we cannot destroy it except by destroying ourselves. We are called to

one great fellowship of love
Throughout the whole wide earth.

And just because we are thus called

Who serves my Father as a son
Is surely kin to me[5]

The key, though, is obedience. "He (or she) who obeys." The key to obedience in turn is love, as Jesus said in another place. "If you love me, you will keep my commandments" (John 14:15). But if we don't, we shan't. The reverse of that is, if we do not keep his commandments, it is because we do not love, or do not love enough. It is so, I submit, in the dearest of human relationships. When I obey my church or my nation or my conscience, it is because I have found something therein to love, something to which I deeply wish to give myself, unequivocally and unreservedly.

In this case, though (I mean in the brotherly case of which Christ speaks) it is not just to *anything* but to the will of God that we give ourselves. That may not, probably will not, be easy or easy to discern. It requires a becoming modesty about how clearly we have identified and understood the will of God. It also entails a becoming readiness to commit ourselves to that will, however dimly discerned.

About all we can be sure of in faith is that it is a

[5] John Oxenham, "In Christ There Is No East or West."

heavenly will and thus that it transcends and judges our own. Human self-interest is so pesky and persistent that we do well to suspect any too easy or too complete identification of our will with the will of our heavenly Father. But that finally is the ground of our hope and confidence. Ultimately, because we know Jesus, we also know that the heavenly will is a fatherly one. However fractionally we may fulfill it, we rest in the confidence and labor in the certainty that the Father loves us even more, infinitely more, than we love ourselves—and that is plenty. When that is the will we seek to discover, and when that is the will we endeavor to do, we shall also discover, in the doing of it, our brothers and sisters.

IV

What all this implies, I hope you see, is that we belong to a universal human family. Moreover, if we see it as less than universal, we undermine and ultimately destroy its nature as family. Either all of us belong to it or none of us does, fully.

Of course there are families within the family, just as there are separate but related neighborhoods within a town. We cannot be related equally intensely to all. But the intimacy of my relationship to my smaller family stands as token and reminder of my extensive relationships to all of God's children.

Let me try an example. I have had reason of late to reflect with special force and frequency upon my relationship with my father, upon the ties that bind us together. Not all these ties are physical of course. These, dear though they be, are not even the most important. He is not only my father in the flesh but my father in the gospel and my brother in the ministry. Each of these relationships is a little different, though a part of the whole. I rejoice that he who gave me life also introduced me to the Lord of life. I am grateful that he gifted me not only with the blood that courses in my veins but also with the faith that beats in my heart. Because he gave me this, in the special intimacy of a family and a faith, I am bound in faith to brothers and sisters in the larger family of humankind.

Antoine de Saint-Exupéry has a finely sculpted passage in his *Flight to Arras*. "I understand," he says, "the origin of brotherhood among men. Men were brothers in God. One can be a brother only *in* something. Where there is no tie that binds men, men are not united but merely lined up. . . . The pilots of Group 2-33 are brothers in the Group. Frenchmen are brothers in France."[6]

So we are brothers and sisters in Christ. And it is finally in that "in Christ" that the family we are and are to become has point and permanence. For here we learn to discern and are empowered to do that divine will which ties us together and makes us one.

Or remember how another great Frenchman put it.

6 *Flight to Arras* (New York: Reynal & Hitchcock, 1942), p. 239.

Pierre Teilhard de Chardin says it unforgettably: "Someday, after we have mastered the winds, the waves, the tides and gravity, we will harness for God the energies of love, and then—for the second time in the history of the world—men will have discovered fire." "Therefore"—so the book of Hebrews—"let us be grateful for receiving a kingdom that cannot be shaken, and thus let us offer to God acceptable worship, with reverence and awe; for our God is a consuming fire" (12:28-29).

Chapter III

THE QUESTION OF GOODNESS
"What More Are You Doing Than Others?"
(MATTHEW 5:47b) *Luke 6:3𝑥*

At our house we chuckled one morning at a story included in breakfast-table devotions. A small boy, living on a farm, had been cautioned by his grandmother against engaging in what she called "worldly amusements" on Sunday. Sadly the boy surveyed his little collection of thus forbidden objects: his basketball, his air rifle, his fishing rod. Dejected and lonely he decided to take a walk down the lane. As he leaned against a fence along the lane, a mule came up, nuzzled the little guy with his big soft nose, rubbed against him with his long sad face. Finally the lad sighed and said to the mule, "Poor fellow, you must be Christian, too."

As we said at the beginning of chapter 1, goodness has very easily and rather frequently been given a bad name, as reflected also in the little girl's prayer, "O Lord, make the bad people good, and *please* make the good people happy." Numerous writers have tried to correct that imbalance by examining some of the ways in which goodness has clumsily sprained its ankle. In this chapter I want to attempt something more positive than that. I want to attend to what Jesus said and, even more, to what he implied, about the question of goodness.

Before that, though, a warning, or maybe a literary self-defense. Recall the conversation of the always-questioning Socrates with a young grad of the Athens Military Academy. The youthful Hellenic "shavetail" was relating how his instructor at the academy had advised him that, in battle, he should station the best men in the front and in the rear ranks and the worst men in the center. "Well and good," said Socrates (which, for Socrates, sometimes meant: not so well and not very good) "but did your teacher teach you how to tell the good men from the bad?" When the embarrassed reply was, "No," the Gadfly of Athens bit back, "Then you'd better go and get your money back." Fair, and fair warning, if by chance the reader needed it. I offer no money-back guarantee that what I am going to suggest herein will certainly enable anyone to divide the good gals and guys from the bad.

I

Jesus commenced, rather strangely, by saying, "In olden times you have heard that they said, 'You must love your neighbor but hate your enemy'" (Matthew 5:43).

I say, "rather strangely," because, as some Jewish commentators have rightly pointed out, the law never *commanded* hatred of the enemy. Way back in the book of Exodus kindness, even to an enemy's animals, was enjoined: "When you come upon your enemy's ox or ass straying, you shall take it back to him. When you see the ass of someone who hates you lying helpless under its load, however unwilling you may be to help it, you must give him a hand with it" (23:4-5 NEB). In contrast to this, when the American Friends Service Committee and others were attempting to garner hospital supplies for victims of the Vietnamese War, North and South, some people reacted as if compassion were a twin brother to treason, as if bandages were good or bad depending upon whose wounds they are wrapped around. I point this out in order to warn against any facile assumption of moral superiority. Centuries ago, Hebrews were treating their enemies' animals better than some of us, in the twentieth century, have thought it appropriate to treat our enemies.

Even though it was not formally taught in times of old, yet clearly it was often said that people should love their neighbors but hate their enemies. In the history of the people out of which Jesus came, ideas and attitudes evolved, including ideas like "neighbor" and "enemy." At lower, less developed levels hostility or even retaliation was permitted or encouraged. Even the psalmists, whose reverence is sometimes yoked and matched with retribution, are able to cry out against those they counted the adversaries of God:

> I hate them with perfect hatred;
> I count them my enemies. (139:22)

They had not been *commanded* so to hate. Nevertheless they hated.

How it was, or was seen, by Hebrews of old is, however, quite beside the Christian point. We shall never even begin to understand the *Sermon on the Mount* unless we accept that it *was addressed to Christian disciples—and to no one else.* Oh, it has implications for others, if they choose to notice them. But the difficulties therein—the hard demands—are difficult and hard because they presuppose that Jesus is talking to those who propose to call themselves his people, to respond to his commands, to answer his demands—*even if nobody else does.* Comparative religion is a legitimate subject of study, but comparative ethics is not a legitimate standard of measurement for Christians. It may be that others profess less or even, perhaps, perform less. No matter! Jesus is not talking about others, or to them. He is talking to his men and women. So, though this or that *was* said in olden times, nevertheless, "*Now* I say to *you.*"

And what he said, remember, was:

Love your enemies, bless those who insult you, return goodness for hatred, and pray for those who injure you by using you. . . . What special credit do you expect if you love only those who love you? . . . Or, if, like certain pagans, you exchange greetings only within your own circle, what are you doing more than others? Your goodness must have no limits, exactly as your heavenly Father's goodness knows no bounds. (Matthew 5:44, 46-49; my translation.)

II

In order to avoid as much confusion as possible it is important to iterate a quite crucial distinction between loving and liking. I realize it has been said many times before, but the very frequency with which we ignore the distinction argues that it must be made again and again. To draw the difference a bit too finely (for there are overlaps between them), loving has to do with good will, liking with good feelings. We may, usually we do, feel some affection toward someone we like. Jesus clearly was not, and could not have been, saying, Feel good toward your enemies, toward those who insult and hate you. That would be at least dishonest and probably impossible. Try this on as a working definition of the kind of love the Lord is commanding here: *Love is steady desire and sturdy effort directed toward the total well-being of another.* That is a bit formal, to be sure, but at least it takes the emphasis off of our subjective reaction. If somebody is trying to do you in, you cannot be expected to cheer him on or to thank him, but you are expected, as a Christian, to will and work for what is best for him.

That is, you are expected to "bless those who insult you." Interestingly, both the word "bless" and the word "bleed" have the same old English root. So it is:

to bless one who has wronged you may require you to bleed for him, to suffer for her, to sacrifice for them. This is a very great deal of what the Cross of Jesus Christ meant, and means, for blessing one's abusers involves one, each time, in a mini-crucifixion.

Another linguistic clue to the meaning of blessing is freshened by the fact that in Hebrew the word for blessing and the word for waterwell is the same word (BRKH). You can understand this best if you think of yourself as the offender. To be blessed by one you have offended is like receiving a cup of cold water when you anticipated and deserved a cup of gall, or no cup at all. It is to be refreshed when you expected to be rebuked. That, says Jesus, is what is expected of those who are known by his name, marked by his mercy, and blessed with his grace.

This is of a piece with the prayers the good person is to offer for those who "injure you by using you." I insist that we pause at this altar a little longer. No sin is more grave and no offense more degrading than that of using another person, as if that person were merely an instrument, a mechanism, or a means. When we reflect upon what made Jesus angry, we rediscover that it was very often the treating of persons as things: handling women as if they were stimuli or receptacles; treating children as chattels; mistreating foreigners as if they were unimportant because they were unknown. To use another person is nearly always to abuse and injure that person. It is to drag sex down to the level of lust; it is to treat employees as functions or functionaries (just "hands" as we say on the farm); it is to twist ideals into ideology; and, when persons cease to be of any use to our politics or program, it is to lay them aside like outworn or unlaundered garments. Much of the tragedy and most of the sin involved in our continuing governmental unpleasantness lies not in the dollars purloined or in the taxes avoided or in the records altered. It lies in the cynical treatment of persons as if they were simply briefcases for carting money, or computers for storing damaging information, or microphones for broadcasting it. That is, the tragedy lies in treating people as objects to be used or laid aside according to the dictates of caprice or the priorities of desire.

Nevertheless, said Jesus, even if these things are done to us, we are to bless, return goodness, and pray for the perpetrators of evil—all very positive and creative responses to essentially negative and destructive incitements. Indeed, if we were to do what Jesus here enjoins toward our enemies, the practical result would almost amount to having no more enemies to bless, forgive, and pray for.

Why are we called to such extraordinary behavior? Because of whose children we are, namely, the heavenly Father's. Blessing, goodness, and prayer are normative for us children because they are characteristic of our Father. He "makes his sun rise on good and bad alike, and sends the rain on the honest and the dishonest" (Matthew 5:45 NEB). Our panicky prayers in times of peril may betray our disbelief in such even-handed fairness, but that does not wipe out the divine fact. Pious farmers receive no more rain than do infidels. The sun shines upon the evil quite as regularly and just as long as upon the good. All people are God's sons and daughters, but we who *know* ourselves to be his children, and who rejoice in that saving fact, have no responsible choice except to act like it.

That is the reason beneath our Lord's devastating question and comment, "What special credit do you expect if you love only those who love you? Even the tax collectors do that much!" It would be tempting to wander a bit, and to wonder a little, about how, in the 1970s, we are supposed to love the Internal Revenue Service. I shall resist that temptation except to observe that the lordly law of love is not satisfied by reciprocal trade agreements: not fulfilled by attitudes like, "You understand my problem and I'll try to understand yours. You massage my ache and I'll rub yours." Rather, Jesus was saying, *my people are obliged to understand even if they are misunderstood, to comfort even if they are undercut.* Besides, Jesus was not thinking of bureaucracies like the Israelite Revenue Service. He was thinking of old Jake, who sat there at the tax desk and who, for all his failings and compromises and readiness to have his palm greased, was nevertheless—and in spite of all that— a human being who should, from us, get better than he had given.

Now Jesus moves to a different illustration of the same hard truth. "If . . . you exchange greetings only within your own circle, what are you doing more than others?" I feel obliged to observe here that even this might be some advance (I mean, really greeting those within our own circles). As a pastor few things distress me more than the way in which Christians permit other allegiances, alliances, and loyalties to divide them from fellow Christians. I know of no gospel reason why political liberals and political conservatives should find fellowship a problem between them, providing they remember first who they are, namely, brothers and sisters in Christ.

politics

Quite so. But not quite enough. Jesus' purpose here is to push us beyond alien categories like "tax collector" or charming categories like "our circle." The danger in the former, alien categories, is that we may fail to recognize how much we have in common with those who are quite unlike us. The danger in the latter, charming categories, is that we may fail to see how easily community can degenerate into cronyism. Jesus does not want his people to be limited by either their prejudices or their preferences.

His point is enfolded in the final verse of this classic passage: "Your goodness must have no limits, exactly as your heavenly Father's goodness knows no bounds" (vs. 48).

In my translation of that I deliberately avoided the usual phrase, "You shall be perfect." I did so because the word "perfect" conveys a rigid, static notion —perfection—which poorly communicates what I think Jesus meant here. Also, and more important, perfection too easily bleeds into perfection*ism*. A perfectionist, someone has well if not too kindly said, is a person who takes infinite pains with everything he does and passes them on to other people. Perfectionists are often unhappy and sometimes unbending people who are seemingly unable to accept either themselves or others as they are.

Yet, despite that, the call remains: "Your goodness must have no limits, exactly as your heavenly Father's goodness knows no bounds." The will of God for us—a goodness without limits—*is* attainable.

III

So, with this as background, let's reach toward a description of goodness. "Goodness . . . is the expression of superabundant life . . . our way of endlessly becoming more and more of what we are, so that other people are enabled to do so also. It is the overflowing of joy—the joy which brings life to everybody it meets."[1]

H. A. Williams, a priest of the Church of England and one of the most insightful of its thinkers, has placed the same truth in a corporate context. He asks:

Why is it now unethical to treat Africans as the best of our grandfathers did? Have we more concern for justice and mercy than Albert Schweitzer? Why is it now unethical to starve strikers into working? Did not St. Paul say: "If any

[1] H. A. Williams, *True Resurrection* (New York: Holt, Rinehart and Winston, 1972), p. 116.

one will not work, let him not eat"? Are we more moral than St. Paul? God forbid. Why is capital punishment now considered by many Christians as unethical when our Christian forefathers considered it the law of God? Are we really nearer to God than they? Why has remarriage after divorce now under certain circumstances earned the blessing of the church, when it was once considered utterly wrong in all circumstances? Why was contraception wrong in 1920 and right now?[2]

The answer, as should be obvious, is that goodness *is* a blessing, an awakening thing, a refreshing thing, a dynamic and therefore a changing thing.

Phillips Brooks, the great Episcopal bishop of the late nineteenth century, was a man to whom many students looked for guidance and in whom many, young and old, found strength. One student tells of seeking and securing an appointment with the bishop in order to consult him on a problem that had long perplexed him. He tells how, with careful thought, he phrased his question in advance so that he would ask it in the best possible way. He spent an engrossing hour with the bishop, but as he walked up Boston's Beacon Street on the way home it occurred to him suddenly that he had not even asked his question. "But," he recorded later, "I did not care. I had found out that what I needed was not the solution of a special problem, but the contagion of a triumphant life."

I wish to witness that in the Goodman from

[2] *Ibid.*, p. 123.

Nazareth, who asked this question of goodness, "What do you more than others?" I have found both: both the solution to many special problems and the contagion of a supremely triumphant life. In him goodness becomes both a requirement and a reward. You may refuse the reward, but you cannot escape the requirement.

What are you doing more than others?

Chapter IV

THE QUESTION OF FEAR
"Why Are You Afraid?"
(MATTHEW 8:26)

The summer before we moved to Illinois, in the early sixties, we vacationed on the Jersey Shore. Being a nautically näive Midwesterner, I blithely and, as it turned out, stupidly took a nine-foot johnboat out into the bay, expecting to do some fishing. Shortly—and very quickly—a storm came up. Before long the only dry thing in the boat was the roof of my mouth. My tackle box was soon floating better than my boat. Trying to row toward shore, when I could see the shore, was like trying to propel the *Queen Elizabeth* with an eggbeater. Though I am a good swimmer, I do not ever remember being so scared. Finally, luckily, the angry waves tossed my little craft up against a seawall. Clinging to the rock, I crawled ashore. "And behold, there arose a great storm on the sea, so that the boat was being swamped by the waves. . . . And he said to them, 'Why are you afraid?'" (Matthew 8:24, 26*a*)

Admittedly there were some important differences between the two crises, not the least of which was that the New Testament boat was filled with apostles whereas mine was not. Nevertheless, if anyone, probably including Jesus, had asked me on that August afternoon why I was afraid, I would have concluded at least that it was an extraordinarily inept, not to say stupid, question, or at best that he knew something I didn't.

As it turned out, in the New Testament case, the latter was the answer: he *did* know something they didn't. But that is to anticipate. In any event, in this chapter we are to deal with another question that Jesus asked, namely, Why are you afraid?

I

If you read this section of Matthew's Gospel with some care, you will discover that this story is actually the first of a trilogy, each part of which attributes to the Lord an unusual power. Here he is described as possessing power over natural forces, specifically over the wind and the waves. In the second, long before William Peter Blatty was even heard of, he is seen as an exorcist, casting demons out of two cave dwellers, no less! In the third he assumes— many of his contemporaries said "presumes"—the power to forgive sins, ordinarily a prerogative thought to belong to God alone. I ask you to note this themethread running through this trilogy, namely, God's power energizing a human person. This basically is what is being affirmed by these recollections, apart from details about stilled seas or chastened demons.

In recent years New Testament scholars have helped us understand that a very great deal of the New Testament is made up of reflections or recollections of the primitive, emerging church (naturally, since these books were all written after the completion of Jesus' ministry. Snatches and fragments were written down within twenty years of Jesus' death; the Gospels themselves several years after that). We are seeing many of these events through second-generation eyes.

Perhaps an analogy will assist us to see the significance of this literary fact. If you read the editorials and assessments made of President Lincoln written during his lifetime, you get a somewhat different picture from the one emerging during the period beginning, say, after 1885. The latter reflects not just immediate impressions but continuing consequences. It emerges in the light of a horribly costly and unbelievably bloody war. It is seen as a result of the amnesty proffered all but about five hundred Confederates. It is felt through the gradually healed wounds of a sutured nation. This 1885 picture of Lincoln is not necessarily less or more accurate than the 1865 picture. But it is nuanced differently.

In a similar way this story from the Gospel of Matthew may be fruitfully understood as the reflections and recollections of a persecuted and frightened group of Christians during the reign of Nero. Nero was not to be the last ruler to believe that philosophy was too impractical a subject for a head of state to study—nor the last to be proved wrong in that belief. He prefaced his Golden House with a colossus bearing what he took to be a likeness of himself, haloed! Then Rome burned, and a hungry, homeless populace sought a corporate scapegoat. While the debauched Emperor may not have encouraged the public ire to turn upon these *Chrestiani,* so named for a long dead rabbi from Nazareth named Jesus, nevertheless he certainly did not restrain it.

Under these circumstances, then, it was no wonder that this tiny Christian band—hunted, haunted, buffeted, and lashed by the storms of imperial ire —should have remembered that sudden storm and the churning lake, the Master's presence and the power he exhibited, the faith he engendered, and the hope he justified. Now hidden in some friendly Roman's home or disguised in servant's garb, now breaking their sacramental bread in clammy catacombs, now awaiting execution in the arena as a part of what their persecutors so cruelly called "games," in all this they were buoyed up and sustained by the reverent memory of a helpless boat and a hellish storm and a helping hand and a voice that said, more in compassion than in judgment, "Why are you afraid?"

One other thing: it would be unfair, in attempting to understand this story, to import twentieth-century questions into a first-century situation. Besides, I do not know the answers, and I doubt if many people do.

I am referring to questions like, How do we *explain* the stilling of the storm? Or, in the sister version in Matthew 14, did, or how did, Jesus walk on the water? While there is a healthy strain of history in the New Testament, its writers did not worship at the shrine of fact. They worshiped at the shrine of Jesus. That is the fact, and that is the significance, we want to try to get at in this chapter, however strangely they formulated or clothed that fact.

II

Thus far I have employed words like "fear" and "afraid" without indicating what should be obvious, namely, that they may be used with a variety of shades of meanings.

Some distinction, though, is necessary, for there are fears and there are fears, good fears and bad ones, holy fears and faithless ones. "Some things," said Aristotle, "it is right and noble to fear and a shame not to fear, disgrace for example." He goes on to describe the brave person as one "who faces and fears the right things, for the right motive, in the right way, and at the right time . . ." (*Nichomachean Ethics*, chapter 9). A healthy fear of fire (or a respect, if you prefer) is essential to the safety of a child. On the other hand, an unhealthy fear of fire, unable to distinguish between firebugs and fireflys, can indicate personality disturbances and personal consequences of a quite serious kind.

Such bad fear, what Berdyaev somewhere called

"the temporary insanity of fear," can be debilitating, immobilizing, frustrating (to oneself and to others). It can lead to the most unrealistic thoughts (though they seem to the one afraid quite real) and to the most irrational acts. It does little or no good to try to assure the person that he should not be afraid, for fear has large eyes, seeing what is not there. You can twist your ankle quite severely on the step that isn't there.

On the other hand, good fear (Aristotle's noble fear) is a preserver of life, of perspective, and of sanity. In battle the best soldiers are not the fearless ones. They may simply be foolhardy. The best soldiers are those who know fear but who can look it in the eye and stare it down. A healthy fear of disgrace is but the other side of a healthy regard for integrity. Many fears are healthy: the fear of disappointing those whom I love or who love me; fear that my church may be embarked upon a course that is unwise, or that my nation may be chartered under a captain who is wrong. This kind of fear, by contrast, can be strengthening, energizing, and fulfilling. Who never fears is unwise; who always fears is undone. Either state is just as bad, and finally just as fearful, as the other.

III

What I have written about the context of the biblical narrative and about the psychological nature of fear is in order to provide a kind of backdrop. Against that backdrop I propose that we look now at what we can learn from the symbolism of this story.

First, is it not true that trouble reveals what we are made of? Some people are shipwrecked before they get aboard, to paraphrase Seneca, who quickly added that adversity is the test of the strong. Actually adversity is the test of the weak, too. It is simply that some of us fail that test. Had you asked the apostles that bright afternoon when, carefree and obedient, they climbed into the boat and headed out for the land of the Gadarenes, they would have told you that of course they had faith. But they would have been able to say that, as events turned out, only because the sky was bright and the lake was calm and all was apparently right with their world. Then came the storm, swooping down upon them, overwashing them, startling them into panic and, withal, revealing what manner of men they were. Arthur John Gossip has a great sermon in which he says very much the same thing with a sober Scottish beauty that defies paraphrase but begs to be quoted:

If you have caught your breath . . . when splashing through the shallow waters of some summer brook, how will you fare when Jordan bursts its banks, and rushes, far as the eye can see, one huge, wild swirl of angry waters, and, your feet caught away, half choked, you are tossed nearer and nearer to the roaring of the falls, and over it?[1]

I think we need not linger long with that thought, except to peer into it and, peering, see how it is

[1] "But When Life Tumbles In—What Then?" in *The Hero in Thy Soul* (New York: Scribner's, 1929), pp. 106-7.

indeed in times of trouble that what we claim to believe is either denied or verified.

When Peter tried to rush to his Lord in what anybody would acknowledge were virtually impossible circumstances, what did him in? Why, what did him in was a simple shift of attention. He shifted his gaze from his Deliverer to his difficulties. That will do it every time. Jeannette Struchen tells in her fine little book on Pope John how one priest informed that great Christian that it would be absolutely impossible to open the (Vatican) Council in 1963. "Fine," said the Pope; "We'll open it in 1962!" [2] The priest's mind was riveted to the obstacles; the Pope's mind was freed by the opportunities. One was mesmerized by his fears; the other was energized by his hopes. How often, how vastly that is true: in the nation and in the home, in the church and in the school, in the loves that bind and bless us or the hostilities that blind and repress us—the difference between a swamped boat and a successful voyage is not in the wind but in the sail.

Jesus called these particular persons, "O men of little faith," (Matthew 8:26) or, as this has been paraphrased, "You half-believers." Notice that, though their belief was only half and halfhearted, his response was not. Jesus is able and willing to accept even our first steps, our tentative commitments, our beginning beliefs, and to give them standing and

---

[2] Jeanette Struchen, *Pope John XXIII: The Gentle Shepherd* (New York: Franklin Watts, 1969), p. 105.

stature. Nobody has to worry because he cannot "believe everything." Who can? Or should? Jesus accepts us where we are, for what we are. Remember this, celebrate this, O ye of little faith. The point is not the size of your faith, little or great. The only question is whether you have offered all of it, large or little, to the Lord of your life.

Notice too the interesting and vital contrast between the phrases, "a great storm" at the beginning of the story and "a great calm" at the end. The difference between them, and the cause of the difference, was the apostolic recognition that Jesus was present. Is this not so? Is not the difference between our turbulence and distress on the one hand and our calm and confidence on the other the simple fact that a Lordly presence has entered to possess and preserve us? Similar people facing similar problems emerge from them dissimilarly. The difference lies not so much in the persons or even in the problems but in him whose Presence they have come to recognize, rejoice in, and respond to. "A great storm . . . a great calm." The difference between them is a difference in faith.

Like the apostles we sometimes assume that we must wake Jesus up else he will not know what is worrying our world. Not so. The Christian faith basically is that "God was in Christ." (II Corinthians 5:19a KJV) If so, his presence broods above us, his care continues round us, his strength remains among us whether we wake or sleep, whether we win or lose. The very gospel of God begins with the Christmas command of the angel, "Fear not" (Luke 2:10 KJV) and climaxes with the apostolic announcement, "Perfect love casts out fear" (I John 4:18). He is here—God with us, Emmanuel—all the while, whether we know it, or want it, or not.

Fundamentally then the answer to the question of fear is interfaced with trust—not belief in spite of evidence but life in scorn of consequences.[3] Notice how our Lord's own life leads us to this conclusion. Nothing about his date with destiny could tempt us to conclude that faith means safety. He prayed for deliverance—but was delivered up. He came to bring life, but suffered a cruelly calculated death. If anyone ever had any reason to expect protection and vindication it was he. Nevertheless

he had no form or comeliness that we should look at him,
  and no beauty that we should desire him.
He was despised and rejected by men;
  A man of sorrows, and acquainted with grief . . .

(Isaiah 53:2*b*, 3*a*)

Yet despite these sorrows and that grief he is able to say, "Fear not . . ." (Matthew 10:31) and "I have overcome . . ." (John 16:33).

All of this is drawn together, beautifully and truly, by an entry in the Scottish psalter. In a paraphrase of the 34th psalm we are taught to sing, of God:

[3] I am vaguely aware of a literary indebtedness here but, if so, have been unable to identify it.

> Fear Him, ye saints, and you will then
> Have nothing else to fear.

Ah yes! It is a question not of whether we fear, but of what we fear—or better, of whom we revere. If beneath it all is a rock-confidence in the God of all creation, then, though many things can disturb, nothing at all can defeat us. For then we shall have learned, with those frightened fishermen in that Galilean boat, that

the sufferings of this present time are not worth comparing with the glory that is to be revealed to us. . . . If God is for us, who is against us? . . . Who shall separate us from the love of Christ? Shall tribulation, or distress, or persecution, . . . or peril, or sword? . . . No, in all these things we are more than conquerors through him who loved us. . . . Neither death, nor life, . . . nor things present, nor things to come, . . . nor anything else in all creation, will be able to separate us from the love of God. . . . (Romans 8:18-39)

That, ere long, was the message they were claiming and proclaiming at the peril of their lives, throughout the world. And that finally is the triumphant answer to the question of fear—for them, for us, for all mankind.

Chapter V

The Question of Identity
"Who Do Men Say That I Am?"
(MATTHEW 16:13)

On the file folders in its biographical morgue *The Washington Post* identifies famous people with a single vocational notation ("home run king," "motion picture star"). One of these . . . is marked "Jesus Christ (martyr)." How *do* you classify him? A *Who's Who* of this era would have had difficulty locating him, since the conventional marks of status were not evident. . . . He had no degrees, no club memberships, no publications, no offspring, no institutional ties, no honors.[1]

How do you classify him?

So we come to this chapter's question from the lips of Jesus, "Who do people say that I am?" (combining Matthew 16:13b and 15).

[1] Martin E. Marty in a book review in *Saturday Review*, September 16, 1967, p. 46.

THE QUESTION OF IDENTITY

I

Their speculation about who he was is hardly sur-
prising. He was being seen more and more, and with
more and more people, along the roads, on the hill-
sides, and in the towns. Some, even among his critics,
called him a "Good Teacher," though his credentials
as a rabbi were irregular to say the least. It is ex-
tremely doubtful whether, nowadays, he would be
awarded tenure in the Division of Religious Studies
in, say, the University of Illinois. Strange
psychosomatic events were taking place quite regularly at his hand, and he had been heard to refer to
himself as a physician (Matthew 9:12, passim). Yet,
again, the Galilean Medical Association did not and
probably would not list him among its members.
Others had commenced to call him by even stronger
titles, like king. Enthusiasm, both popular and private, was reaching such a pitch that, ere long, a
woman would anoint his head with oil, quite as kings
are anointed, and crowds would gather to greet his
entry into the Holy City of Jerusalem just as if he were
a ruling monarch. Under these emerging circumstances, I say, it is quite natural that the question
should multiply itself on many lips, "Just who *is* he
anyway?"

Just now Jesus and the Twelve are in the city earlier
called Paneas for the god Pan, more recently bearing
the compound name Caesarea Philippi for Caesar and

his local functionary, the Tetrarch Philip.[2] The city was situated at the foot of the Lebanon range. It was a beautiful and notable community. Here, amidst the reminders of pagan splendor and Roman power, Jesus, for some reason, indulged himself in that very human question, "What do people think of me?" or, as Mark phrases it, "Who do men say that I am?" (8:27)

Like most friends, they do not tell him immediately what *they* think. Rather, they repeat the rumors, what the grapevine says. One version had it that he was John the Baptizer (the local authorities were superstitiously frantic lest the recently executed John should return to haunt them). Others, with more insight, thought he might be Elijah or Jeremiah. Interesting guesses all, illuminating as they do the impression Jesus made on his contemporaries: John the Baptist, fiery-tongued denouncer of spiritual complacency and self-righteousness. Elijah: fierce critic of false worship; Elijah, who, like Jesus, had spent forty days in his wilderness on Mt. Horeb and had challenged his wishy-washy, limping people, "If the Lord be God, follow him" (I Kings 18:21 KJV). Jeremiah, the most Christ-like figure in the Old Testament, who met with opposition from princes, priests, and people and who

[2]In this and the following paragraph I have adapted a few sentences that originally appeared in an earlier book. Ernest J. Fiedler and R. Benjamin Garrison, *The Sacraments: An Experiment in Ecumenical Honesty* (Nashville: Abingdon Press; and Notre Dame, Ind.: Fides Publishers, 1969), pp. 113,114.

was opposed by his homefolk. These guesses shed light on what people were seeing in Jesus because all three of these were "men of fearless courage, singular devotion, unflinching loyalty to high ideals . . . great simplicity and stern self-discipline."[3]

Now, however, Jesus turns away from the "they" question to the "you" question. He asks Peter, "But you, Peter, who do *you* say that I am?" Before we deal with the big fisherman's answer, I ask you to remember what the contrast between these two questions implies. It implies that Jesus understood and accepted the fact that there would be a difference between what "others" thought and what brothers thought of him.

It is a mark and measure of Jesus' meaning and influence in history that nearly everybody feels obliged or entitled to have an opinion about him. Even those who have chosen to try to dismiss him are tacitly admitting that he is a factor to be contended with. Jesus has been denounced. He has been patronized. He has been praised even when he is not served. He has been cursed, criticized, and categorized. Both in his own time and since he has been called a madman, a pretender, a blasphemer.

I do not by this language mean to imply that all or even most of the judgments about Jesus by outsiders are unfair or unfriendly. Quite to the contrary, some

---

[3] *The Abingdon Bible Commentary* (New York and Nashville: Abingdon Press, 1929), p. 980b.

of them have been strikingly appreciative and affirmative. For instance, one of the distinguished Anglo-Jews earlier in this century was an able scholar named Claude Montefiore. He remarked what he called "the originality of Jesus" in the following tribute: "Through the Gospel mists and miracles, a character seems to emerge in many respects unlike *any* Old Testament . . . teacher or saint."[4]

(My points are two: First, running clean from the New Testament to our time, judgments about Jesus have varied from admiring to hostile. Second, Jesus early perceived that the judgment of his friends and followers would differ sharply from the judgments of more or less neutral bystanders or active opponents.)

Still, whatever others thought or said, the Master would not excuse Peter, and does not excuse us, from a personal assessment, a personal judgment, and a personal response. Peter could not evade or postpone or quote or equivocate. When those piercing eyes looked at him and that compelling voice spoke to him, Peter had to decide where he himself stood, and that right quickly. So he exclaimed, in words that have become classic in Christian confession, "Thou art the Christ, the Son of the living God!" (Matthew 16:16 KJV).

What lay beneath this affirmation, what it implied about the subtle and saving relationship between the

---

[4] In *Contemporary Thinking About Jesus,* compiled by Thomas S. Kepler (New York and Nashville: Abingdon-Cokesbury Press, 1944),p. 379.

Lord of the universe and this carpenter-peasant-rabbi from the hills of Galilee—all of this would be a long time getting expressed with any clarity, consistency, or completeness. Dr. Fosdick, one of the great preachers of this century, helpfully suggests the process through which the young church grew in its certitude about the identity of its leader as Lord. He says:

At first they may have said, God sent him. After a while that sounded too cold, as though God were a bow and Jesus the arrow. That would not do. God did more than send him. So . . . they went on to say, God is with him. That went deeper. Yet, as their experience with him progressed, it was not adequate. God was more than with him. So at last we catch the reverent accents of a new conviction. God came in him. That was not so much theology at first as poetry. It was an exhilarating insight and its natural expression was a song.[5]

I think we need not debate, and in any case cannot settle, the question of how many of these claims made *for* Jesus were also made *by* him. That, in Dr. Montefiore's phrase, is lost in the "Gospel mists." Yet quite apart from the details of it, the terms and titles and vocabulary—Messiah, Son of God, Lord—one thing is clear, even through the mists: Jesus conducted himself in such a way that he staked out at least an indirect claim on the realities and relationships his followers claimed in his name. He quietly assumed to be speaking a later word from God: "But *I* say unto you." He repeatedly demanded complete loyalty. "Come, leave, take up, follow." It is almost axiomatic

[5] H. E. Fosdick, *Living Under Tension* (New York: Harper, 1941), p. 156.

that a person cannot become fully mature or completely creative unless he knows himself, knows who he is. Jesus surely passed that test. He knew the answer to his own question about who he was.

II

Just as Peter could not avoid Jesus' second question, neither can we. Christians are obliged to answer "Who do you say that I am?" no matter what others think or do not think, believe or decline to believe, about him. That this can, and sometimes does, result in special pleading may not be denied. But, even as we acknowledge this risk, it must be taken, else we should be forced up against "the perverse conclusion . . . that everyone has a right to a verdict on Jesus except those who know most about him" (*Interpreter's Bible*, VII, 765b).

What has to be avoided, if you have really *heard* Jesus asking *you* his question, is what might be called a "term-paper attitude" toward Jesus. Recently, in order to remind myself of what that means, I got out one of my old undergraduate term papers, just for fun. Thus endeth the fun. It was titled, ponderously, "A Comparison of the Philosophies of William James and Henri Bergson" (in 16½ pages yet!). It included an impressive eleven-item bibliography, incorrectly listed. It was obese and breathless with 30 quotations, or 1.88 quotations per page. It was cloyed and bloated with such exciting phrases as "It has been asserted" and such freshly minted ones as "from time im-

memorial." If there had been an original idea in it
(which there was not), that idea would have died from
solitary confinement. And as for what I thought about
William James or Henri Bergson or radical empiri-
cism, I gave my professor not a clue (which omission
made the B he gave me a testimony to the triumph of
generosity over judgment).

That is what I mean by a term-paper attitude, and
that is precisely what cannot be meant or permitted in
the Christian's attitude toward Christ. Footnotes are,
of course, allowed. This is one of the functions of
creeds, Bible texts, and Christian history. Christian
faith did not begin the day you or I achieved it. But at
some point—and this is the vital point—I am obliged
to put myself on the line with a decision, a declara-
tion, an "include me in" or "count me out" that trans-
forms the whole enterprise from the academic to the
existential. The only way to hand in an answer to the
Lord's question is to hand over myself. It is not a term
paper but a personal application, no longer blank, for
it has my name written upon it.

The way to act *responsibly* as a Christian is to act
responsively, that is, to respond. Then, responding,
we shall begin to see with a new clarity, and to feel
with a new intensity, that this Gospel Figure meets,
matches, and surpasses every expectation we could
have had. Let me ask, Who could be for you a Savior?
Speaking for myself, yet not for myself alone, I have
found that question more than answered in Jesus
whom we call the Christ. He is sovereign yet neigh-

borly. He is zealous yet tranquil. He is austere yet compassionate. He is demanding yet forgiving. Name me a noble human quality, and I shall show you that quality, live and luminous, in him. Name me a god-like quality and, again, I shall point you toward it, in him.

Dr. W. Russell Hindmarsh, professor of atomic physics, has written of his responses to studying the thought of Albert Einstein. He says that the sheer power of the mind of Einstein, and the depth of his understanding, was simply overwhelming. It produced the same effect as one's first sight of England's Durham Cathedral or as hearing again Beethoven's Ninth Symphony. To this observation he added, "It is something to belong to the same race of beings as Einstein." Indeed it *is* something, thrilling and almost inexpressible. But think now, you who name the Name of Christ, what it means to belong to the same race of beings as Jesus Christ—an even greater thing.

To belong to this race, though (or better, to belong to this community) does not eliminate the element of venture. As we look at him, we listen to him. As we respond to him there is enough in what he discloses about God "to warrant our venture, but never enough to spare us the venture" (*Interpreter's Bible*, VII, 451b).

The central venture of Christian faith is that Jesus Christ is God's idea. I know that is not the usual way of putting it, so let us pause here and ponder. Professor Merrill Abbey, one of America's ablest teachers of preachers, has pointed out the delightful ambiguity in the phrase "conceived by the Holy Spirit."[6] Con-ceived can mean "to become pregnant with." But it can also mean "to think or to form an idea." So Jesus, however else we may understand or fail to understand him, was God's idea. As the Great God of all creation brooded over his world, as he pondered how to make clear and convincing his will and way, an idea began to take shape, and to take the shape of a person. That idea "became flesh and dwelt among us, full of grace and truth." (John 1:14). I am not suggesting that this way of putting it is equatable with what the early church meant when it said that Christ was "conceived by the Holy Spirit." I am suggesting that this way of putting it is *consistent* with their way: Jesus as God's idea—here by God's purposing, ours by God's de-sign, an earth dweller with a heavenly source, thought into our lives and sent into our midst by the explicit will of God.

So, as I look back upon it now, *The Washington Post* is right, however inadvertently. The file folder "Jesus Christ, martyr" is quite accurate, if we remember that "martyr" means "witness." For Jesus Christ witnesses to the tremendous and tumultuous love of God; to the care with which he created, and the concern with which he follows, the earth and them that dwell therein. Jesus Christ witnesses, as none before or none yet, to the saving, sovereign fact that love is stronger than death, that life is more than breath, and

[6] Merrill R. Abbey, *The Shape of The Gospel* (Nashville: Abingdon Press, 1970), p. 26.

that we are "born anew to a living hope" (I Peter 1:3): Jesus Christ, God's martyr, our witness, and therefore "the ground of our hope, and the promise of our deliverance."

One dark Army night thirty years ago the 51st Signal Operations Battalion was on bivouac. The sky was like India ink. The atmosphere was like a sauna bath. Then, from our pup tent, it was plain to see, despite the darkness, that something out there was on the move. The pine trees began slowly to squirm in the marsh, like nervous witnesses in court. A breeze came up, retreated, and then returned as a full-grown wind. Then, of a sudden, the lightning flashed. In that instant I could see the mess tent over yonder, Corporal Ogden on guard, and the company jeep keeping sleepy watch on the edge of the hill. One minute seemingly impenetrable darkness; the next instant, unbelievable brightness. And then the darkness again.

I suggest, in all reverence, that the revelation in Christ is like that. Nothing, it would seem, can penetrate our darkness or mitigate our night. Then, of a sudden, God caused a Christ-flash to cross our sky. The landscape, a bit ago so frightening and unknown, is for a moment luminescent and clear. So, though the darkness returns, it is no longer an empty darkness. For now we know we are not alone.

"In him was life, and the life was the light of men. The light shines in the darkness, and the darkness has not overcome it." (John 1:4-5.)

Chapter VI

THE QUESTION OF SUFFERING
"My God, Why Hast Thou Forsaken Me?"
(MATTHEW 27:46)

Have you ever felt utterly alone—completely deserted, cut off from everything and everybody? Or, worse, have you ever felt completely deserted and cut off from God? I suspect I can guess the answer of many of my readers. If my guess is accurate, I imagine they feel uneasy and maybe even a little guilty about it.

But, if that includes you, you should not and need not feel uneasy or guilty. You are in good company. The best actually, namely, the company of Jesus: he too felt deserted by God, left lonely and alone to cope if he could or collapse if he couldn't, with no God to hear or help. Anyhow, that is what I understand to be meant by this question Jesus asked—this anguish he hurtled against a senseless sky, "My God, my God, why has thou forsaken me?" (Matthew 27:46)

I

I think we can agree that this is a question the early church absolutely would not have invented or imagined. It was almost unspeakably embarrassing for them to have to admit that these words had escaped the lips of Jesus—so embarrassing, indeed, that Luke had a convenient lapse of memory and so neglected to record this cry as a part of his account of the crucifixion. No, whatever legitimate questions we may have about whether Jesus actually said thus and so or did this or that, *this* word rings with clumsy authenticity. This is something they surely would have preferred to forget, like their own failures in faith and denials and betrayal. Remembering it was like admitting that Honest Abe once lied or that some brave general turned tail in battle and fled. It was, or seemed, so unlike him. Yet there it is: "My God, why have you forsaken me?"

Of course several reasons can be adduced for his defection, some of them pretty good reasons.

For one thing, he had suffered the derision of the crowd. It is no fun to be made the butt of laughter. Moreover, and worse, they derided not just him (that was doubtless not new to him) but they deprecated his mission. "*If* you are the Son of God, come down from the cross" (27:40). Even across the centuries and from a distance we can still hear the sneer in that "if." Poor chap, they were saying, he must have been taken in by all that palm-waving and messiah-talk. Didn't he know that this was all holiday enthusiasm? We didn't really mean what we said last Sunday, but apparently he thought we did. He'd obviously begun to believe his own press clippings. "Son of God" indeed!

In addition to the derision of the crowd was the mockery of the elite: the chief priests, lawyers, and elders. In fact this upper-crust contempt was even worse. These reverends and esquires and sirs talked *about* him without speaking to him, much as contemptuous and condescending adults sometimes speak about children as if the children were not there to hear and be hurt. "Johnnie is really a very naughty boy, don't you think? I do wish he'd grow up." So here. "He saved others," they stage-whispered within earshot. "He cannot save himself. He is the King of Israel, let him come down from the cross, and we will believe in him" (vs. 42). He trusts in God? O.K., let God deliver him. Such sarcasm must have been triply difficult for Jesus to bear because that was something of which he himself was never guilty. Even when his eyes flared with indignation and his voice rose in anger, his lips never curled in contempt or sarcasm. The same cannot be said of his distinguished detractors.

Then, as if these were not quite enough, he was reviled by the common criminals who were being crucified with him. "How the mighty is fallen! He's just like us after all, this 'righteous' rabbi, this 'royal' pretender. We're not saints, but then we never pretended to be. Look at him: just like us when it comes right down to it."

This cry, "My God why?" is quite understandable if only in terms of the vile treatment that spewed from the lips of those around him.

II

The difficulty is augmented by the fact that what Jesus was feeling did not come just from the inhumane treatment of humans. Otherwise he would have said, "O fickle crowds, O establishment priests and lawyers, O convicted criminals, why have you forsaken me?" Rather his questioning cry indicted God himself. One scholar wrote years ago that "in the entire Bible there is no other sentence so difficult to explain."[1] I am not about to rush in where scholars fear to tread, but I must ease in, however cautiously.

At the very least it was a cry of discouragement, of dis/couragement, which means being deprived of one's heart. His ministry had not been long nor long in getting into trouble. Even his mother (who supposedly had received a direct revelation from God, telling her that she was to give birth to "the Son of the Most High" [Luke 1:32]), even she misunderstood his mission and probably even doubted his sanity. His words had been twisted. His motives had been doubted. His days had been crowded with people

[1] James Stalker, quoted by James T. Cleland in *He Died as He Lived* (Nashville: Abingdon Press, 1966), p. 41.

who wanted something from him: a healing, a hearing, a short-cut to salvation, a blessing for their bargain-basement dreams. The enthusiasm of the crowds, that heady mead that ferments so fast, was now bitter to the taste. All of this was enough to discourage any man, even the Son of Man. And it did.

No wonder then, too, that it was a cry of desertion. Where were they whose lives had crisscrossed his and who had seemed so moved and altered by the crossing? Where were they *now?* Where? Where was Matthew, the IRS agent turned apostle, who had found at that vital intersection a new integrity? Where was the Woman at the Well, who had been treated by him as a person for the first time in her tawdry life? Where was Zacchaeus, that runty little rich man, who had met in Jesus at least one, at last, who valued him as a man rather than as a man of means? Indeed at this point, I hazard the guess, Jesus felt so utterly deserted that he would even have welcomed a glimpse of Judas. For Judas, despite his murky ambitions and house-of-mirror goals, had at least the honesty to act upon his wrongness. But it was not to be. Deserted. Alone. Utterly alone.

This lonely, piercing cry has also been called a cry of dereliction. Rightly. In the spring of 1974 the majestic ship *Queen Elizabeth II* was crippled at sea. Yet, strangely, an almost party atmosphere prevailed aboard, at least for a couple of days. That fact, however, should not blind us to the fact that a derelict vessel is no laughing matter. A "wholly forsaken or abandoned" ship is dangerous in its very dereliction: directionless, smashed by the winds, caught by the waves, tossed by the latest and strongest force, unable either to resume or return. It is in this sense that Jesus' anguished cry was a cry of dereliction. He might have been able to take the disembarking of the passengers, however leaky he knew their moral lifeboats to be. But now he felt himself abandoned by the Captain himself, by God. Now he was really alone, utterly, ultimately, and, for all he knew, everlastingly alone. Hence he flung his awful "Why" against the deaf and unanswering sky.

All of which combined to make this desperate cry a cry of doubt. What if these wagging heads and mocking tongues were right? What if he were wrong, despite his single-minded obedience? What if it was all for nothing that he had alienated his family, upset his friends, and called upon his apostles to leave all—for a worse-than-nothing, for an illusion? What if he had come to this City of his fathers and cleansed its Temple and angered its rulers all for naught? He had now risked everything in one great redemptive toss. But what if it were merely a losing gamble, with not an iota of redemption in it for anyone? What if . . . What if . . . "O God, why?"

Yet despite the discouragement, the desertion, the dereliction, and the doubt, his was not a cry of despair. Even at this abysmal moment in his soul, he formed his lips once more around those syllables which every reverent Jew spoke with caution: "Eloi,

Eloi"—God. Even though he believed that God had deserted him, still it was *God* who had deserted him. Despair is the "most self-centered of all emotions." [2] That, even in death, Jesus was not.

Nor was he disillusioned, for the very simple reason that he had no illusions about either humanity or divinity. The former, humanity, he knew to be both the "pride and refuse of the universe."[3] Hence, though he was sad, he was not disillusioned when the moral breath of these men and women stank like garbage. As for the latter, God, Jesus had never expected or supposed that deity, in order to be deity, had to organize itself around his needs or to be determined by his desires. Disappointment, as dark and terrible as ever man felt—yes; disillusionment—no.

Objections have been raised against this passage of scripture by asking whether it is reasonable to believe that a dying man would start quoting, as Jesus is doing here from the twenty-second Psalm. The answer, I should suppose, is that what a person does at death depends largely upon what has been normative and controlling in life. John Wesley, on his deathbed, roused his feeble voice to sing once more Isaac Watts' hymn:

> I'll praise my Maker while I've the breath;
> And when my voice is lost in death,
> Praise shall employ my nobler powers.

[2] K. E. Kirk, *The Vision of God* (London: Longmans Green and Co., 1931), p. 134.
[3] Blaise Pascal, *Pensees. The Provencial Letters.*

An old Scot, in similar straits, called to his spouse, "Reik me the Buek," knowing she would know that "the Book" could refer only to the Bible he had lived with and now proposed to die by. We may perhaps be permitted surprise that Jesus did not quote from, say, the twenty-third Psalm, with its companying words, "Yea, though I walk through the valley of the shadow of death, I will fear no evil" (KJV). But that he quoted from the Psalms is consonant with all we know about him.

Besides, heed from what he quoted. This Psalm has been studied with great care, much as we might look with new eyes at a poem or a book or a painting dear to one dear to us. With these new eyes (I mean with eyes that have also looked upon the Cross) Christians have found some Christ-shaped stanzas. Listen:

> All who see me mock at me, . . .
> they wag their heads;
> [saying] "He committed his cause to the Lord;
> let him deliver him . . ." (Vss. 7, 8)

(They had already taunted him with that).

> They divide my garments among them,
> and for my raiment they cast lots.
> (Vs. 18)

There is more, setting the "why" cry in a context of affirmation and trust. Again, listen:

> Upon thee was I cast from my birth,
> and since my mother bore me thou hast been
> my God. . . .

I will tell of thy name to my brethren; . . .
  I will praise thee. . . .
For [you have] not despised or abhorred
  the affliction of the afflicted;
. . . not hid [your] face from him,
  but [have] heard, when he cried to [you].
(Vss. 10, 22, 24)

Jesus trusted, his very trusting deepening his pain and suffering. He cried, and his very shriek in the void was more piercing because he believed it was God's void.

III

Let us go back to that sarcasm which Jesus found so hard to bear, because he was himself innocent of it. The root of the word means "to tear the flesh, to bite the lips in rage." The latter meaning (to bite one's own lips) is especially germane, for sarcasm is more than sometimes a matter of self-hatred. Most of us are guilty of it now and again. But when a person is constantly sarcastic one has a right to ask him or her, "What is it really that you dislike so much about yourself?'

In the crucifixion case, whatever their unconscious self-contempt, their sarcasm was inadvertently right: "He saved others; he cannot save himself" (Matthew 27:42*a*). How right they were, though ignorantly. Had they known whereof, or of whom, they spoke, they would have said instead, "He saved others: therefore he could not save himself" (*Interpreter's Bible*, VII, 607b). In Charles Wesley's hymnic word, his is "the Death by which we live." In a reminiscence coming out of World War I, a soldier, about to venture out into no man's land between the battle lines, said to the chaplain, "Pray that I'll get back safely." "I can't do that," the Padre replied. "But I'll go with you." In the Cross Jesus Christ enunciated and lived out that vital principle. You cannot liberate others by holding back yourself. Truly his mockers were right, "Himself he cannot save"—not and be or remain the Christ.

I cannot myself make any sense of the crucifixion or of suffering except in terms of the trusting belief that God himself is involved in what happens there. I am as appalled and repelled as anyone by the supposition that God somehow demanded of his most faithful servant that he, Jesus, render up sufficient suffering so that God's heart would be melted and turned in mercy toward humankind. Rather I prefer the biblical view that "God was in Christ, reconciling" (II Corinthians 5:19 KJV). What happened in and to and through Jesus Christ happened in and to and through God himself. What hurt the Son pained the Father. Thus I believe, and gratefully affirm, with MacLeish's J. B.:

> I do not know why God should strike
> But God is what is stricken also . . .[4]

[4]Archibald MacLeish, *J. B.* (Boston: Houghton Mifflin, 1956), p. 89.

Moreover we need not mystify or over-theologize this. It is just plain, inescapable, human truth. What happens to my children pains or pleases me more than anything that could possibly happen to me alone. I know of no reason under heaven—particularly under Heaven—why this should be less true of God than it is of me.

It is interesting that this literally ex-cruciating word (this word "from the cross") is the only one of the recorded seven that Matthew gives space to. Yet for all the somberness of it, it is important to note, Matthew's Jesus dies as Victor. Luke says, almost blandly, "He [Jesus] breathed his last" (23:46b). Not so Matthew. No, he concludes—climaxes—with the affirmation, "And Jesus . . . *yielded up* his spirit" (27:50).

No one, as Jesus truly said, took his life from him. Rather he yielded it up, freely, voluntarily, and, if not gladly, nevertheless triumphantly. Like a great warrior returned from battle mortally wounded but triumphant, he handed over his life like a mighty sword. In the thick of the battle, he felt quite alone. But not at the last. At the last, triumph—sobered, chastened, wounded, and tested—but triumph still.

George Matheson's great hymn expresses how, in the Cross of Christ, the question of suffering was answered in glad freedom and final victory:

> I give thee back the life I owe,
> That in thine ocean depths its flow
> May richer, fuller be.

SEVEN QUESTIONS JESUS ASKED

O Cross that liftest up my head,
I dare not ask to fly from thee;
I lay in dust life's glory dead,
And from the ground there blossoms red
Life that shall endless be.

Chapter VII

THE ULTIMATE QUESTION
"Why Are You Weeping? Whom Are You Seeking?"
(JOHN 20:15)

Items (quoted verbatim from some of the Fourth Estate's observations during Holy Week): One hundred-sixty golfers from thirty-two schools tee off starting at 7:30 A.M. Friday . . . in the Fourth Annual *Good Friday Golf Tournament* (italics mine).

("Then Pilate took Jesus and scourged him." This item is from the first verse of the nineteenth chapter of the Fourth Gospel.)

Items (from a single page of advertising in the same edition of the newspaper):

EASTER SAVINGS

HUFFY 26-INCH 10-SPEED BIKE
PADDED BLUE SADDLE
$59.88
ULTRASHEER PANTY HOSE,
NUDE HEEL AND SUPERSTRETCH
2PR.   .99
HOLLOW EGGS
.43 bag

there must be some justice in that

81

("And he entered the temple and began to drive out those who sold, saying to them, 'It is written, "My house shall be a house of prayer"; but you have made it a den of robbers'" Luke 19:45-46.)

One can hardly cite these happenings or quote these words without sounding cynical or seeming resentful. I mean to be neither. I mean only to describe the inescapable atmosphere in which Easter is being celebrated in the 1970s.

I

Neither the problem nor its atmosphere is new. On that Aboriginal Easter Day, too, no doubt some people had their golf games, casting lots or throwing discs, or nursing a toothache, pursuing their tremendous trivialities as if nothing else mattered.

I praise it thus negatively because I think we are obliged to acknowledge that *on Easter we are dealing with ourselves and with our Lord and with no one or nothing else.* The *implications* of the Christian faith are public and universal. If they were not, our Lord would never have burdened his friends with the mandate, "Go *therefore* and make disciples of all nations, baptizing . . . teaching" (Matthew 28:19, 20*a*). However the *foundations* of that faith, the events that framed and formed that faith, these were given to the Christian community *in camera,* as the lawyers say: in private. Let us remember that the resurrection appearances occurred only to the followers of Jesus—not to Pilate or

Herod, nor to the soldiers or the Priests, nor to the crowd or the crown.

They found soon that such a gospel, without headline, footnote, or public proof, was terribly difficult to preach. They, like we, were embarrassed by that difficulty, so someone undertook to remove it. In the so-called Gospel of Peter (not a part of our Bible) somebody tried to produce or point to some independent (that is, unfriendly) witnesses to resurrection. I quote part of the crucial passage in the eighth chapter:

And the Elders were afraid and came unto Pilate, entreating him and saying: Give us soldiers that we may watch his sepulchre for three days, lest his disciples come and steal him away. . . . And Pilate gave them Petronius the centurion with soldiers to watch the sepulchre . . . and they pitched a tent there and kept watch. . . . Now in the night whereon the Lord's day dawned, as the soldiers were keeping guard two by two in every watch, there came a great sound in the heaven and *they saw* the heavens opened and two men descend thence. . . . And that stone . . . rolled away of itself and went back to the side. . . . When therefore those *soldiers saw* that, they waked up the centurion and the elders. . . . And *they heard* a voice out of the heavens . . ."[1]

The early church, very wisely, rejected this passage as no proper part of the Christian Bible (realizing as they did and as we must that "the last proceeding of reason is to recognize that there is an infinity of things which are beyond it" [Pascal]).

[1] *The Apocryphal New Testament*, rev. ed. (Oxford: Clarendon Press, 1953), as cited by Leander E. Keck in *Mandate to Witness* (Valley Forge: Judson Press, 1964), p. 67. (Italics Keck's.)

The Resurrection Community neither argues nor defends but affirms and proclaims. The Easter faith is just that: a faith, no more, but—by *God*—nothing less. It is as Christians that we hear these resurrection questions from the lips of our Lord, "Why are you weeping? Whom are you seeking?" (John 20:15).

II

"Why are you weeping?" Strange that. She was weeping for a friend, lost to death. She was weeping too because now, in the early morning, she had discovered a double indignity: the corpse was gone. Stolen by some heartless, callous creature of the night? Taken by friendly hands to a safer place? She knew not. So, her sorrow heightened by outrage and deepened by questions unanswered, she wept.

Tears are the soap of the soul, cleansing us from the clinging grime of grief or guilt. We may be sure that Jesus, in asking this question, did not mean to deny her such cleansing and relief. We may be sure of that because he did not deny the tears of grief to himself. The shortest, and 'most the tenderest, verse in the Bible is the stark statement, "Jesus wept" (John 11:35). The place is the tomb of his dead friend Lazarus. The pain of it and the penetrating sadness of it and the shattering loneliness of it crushed his heart as in a vise. So he wept.

The cause of Mary's grief was real but not ultimate.

Dawn follows upon darkness. The twisted madness of a spring storm will eventually blend into brightness and relax into calm. These analogies are of course not exact, but they are pointers. "Why are you weeping?" The New Testament composers heard that solitary note and, like good musicians, held it in their heads until the song was ready to begin. Then they pitch-piped it for the choirs whose faithful music it was soon theirs to direct. So John, the George Frederick Handel of the New Testament, brought his mighty chorus to a fortissimo of the faith: "God himself will be with them; he will wipe away every tear from their eyes, and death shall be no more, neither shall there be mourning nor crying nor pain any more, for the former things have passed away" (Revelation 21:3*b*-4).

"Why are you weeping?" Like many of the Bible's questions, this one from the Master is addressed not only to the person who first heard it. "Who are my brothers?" "What are you doing more than others?" "Why are you afraid?" As we have seen in earlier chapters, these questions are illuminated by, but not limited to, their biblical context. So here: we too are being asked why we weep.

Some of us are weeping because of our failures. We mess up our book of days with the gummy thumbprints of our clumsiness. Most of us have had days when nothing seems to go right: from the spilled orange juice at the breakfast table, through the curt reply or hurt response to some irritating but well-meant question, right to the unplanned quarrel or undone plan, the day has limped so badly that we are glad to spank it and put it to bed and be done with it. Now imagine that most of your days were like that, or seemed so. Imagine that everything you touched every day turned to ashes. Imagine that the only word you could pronounce successfully was the word failure: loved ones hurt, goals burnt, ideals bent—life askew. Imagine (I know full well that some who read these words do not have to imagine these things), imagine further that much of this failure is of your own making, or unmaking. So far as we weep because these things have come to pass, our weeping may partake of what the scriptures call a "godly sorrow" (II Corinthians 7:10 KJV). That far, our tears are right. They are right, however, only insofar as we are willing to write "terminus" across the page of our failures, because we have come to know in Christ that these "former things have passed away" (Revelation 21:4).

Or, we may weep for those we love. Nor need they be dead to call forth such tears. She (the loved one) hurts or hinders her own best interests but resists both criticism and sympathy with equal recalcitrance. He (the loved one) despite sincere and steady effort can not seem to avoid bumpy roads and detours. They (the loved ones: children, parents, friends) are enwebbed in suffering, and nothing you can do or say or seemingly pray can free them from the web. That is why you weep. Yet, like one's own failures, these trials of our loved ones must finally be given up and given over in trust to One who is able to do for all of us, including them, "above all that we ask or think" (Ephesians 3:20 KJV).

Spiritually speaking, many of these tears persist because we live in Friday's darkness instead of Sunday's light. That is, we live as if this conversation in that Garden had never transpired, as if the Gardener were dead. Stubborn and deep in the human breast lies a kind of latent atheism, a sort of practical unbelief (though, in the long run, it is anything but practical). I mean by that this: although we may sing with Fortunatus, "Welcome, Happy Morning," we act as if our history had skipped from Saturday to Monday, as if the Day of the Lord had never dawned. We may commence our creeds with pristine orthodoxy, "I believe in God the Father Almighty," but we live as though no mightiness governed and no fatherliness guided the world in which we struggle and strive. So of course we weep. It is a lonely business being your own God—and futile and sorrowful, too. That is why we weep.

Easter does not put an end to all this. That is so important to be said, lest we overstate our Christian claims. Our failures are not ended by fiat. Our loved ones are not exempted from pain. Our faith does not become all at once and forever steady and undisturbed. No, Easter does not put an end to all this—but it does put a crown upon it. A great vision in the Revelation of John pictures a heavenly figure, "a woman clothed with the sun, with the moon under her feet, and on her head a crown of twelve stars . . ."

(Revelation 12:1*b*). But then, with scarcely a pause for breath, we are told that "she was with child and she cried out in her pangs of birth, in anguish for delivery" (vs. 2).

That is the way of it, with us, since Easter: anguish—but with birthing as its purpose. Pain, as in pregnancy, but now with a regal, living result, given and guaranteed by the King of kings. That being so, why do we weep?

III

The first question was, "Why are you weeping?" The second: "Whom are you seeking?"

Mary's answer to the latter would have been straightforward. "I am seeking one who is dead." She could have used a variety of other words: one who is dear, compassionate, wise, helpful, hopeful, human—though the verb would have been past tense, for he had been executed on the day before yesterday. She sought the body of a dead man, as her questioner knew.

He knows our answer too, but asks it nonetheless. Whom are we seeking? Some of our answers, however finally inadequate, are not bad answers. Some of us, even on the Day of Resurrection, are seeking a Teacher: a moral guide, a pedagogue who will introduce us into the way of truth. And, superbly though he does that, there is still no reason why we should prefer Jesus as teacher to, say, Socrates. Leander Keck, able New Testament scholar, phrases the issue sharply when he writes that if Jesus is only a teacher, "this is not really good news but merely a Sunday supplement."[2] Surely it is something more than that that we celebrate on Resurrection Day.

Or perhaps we look for a prophet in Jesus. A prophet we will find, on the model of a Jeremiah, the suffering one, or of a Hosea, the forgiving one. Nevertheless again, a number of others have spoken to the people, prophetically, for God, both before and since. Gandhi was a prophet—a very illuminating one. Dom Helder Camara, Roman Catholic Archbishop in Brazil, is a prophet—a very disturbing one.[3] Still if it is a prophet we want, though we can turn toward the Nazarene, we can turn, with equal benefit, toward others.

Or rebel? We are fond of characterizing him as that, too, particularly in our rhetoric. But, though he did upset, undermine, and denounce, the world has had his equal as rebel, too.

All these qualities and characteristics, true though they be, are penultimate. Each is seen, if truly seen, in the light of his Lordship. Because he is our Lord, he has something important to teach us. Because he is our Lord, his prophecy is remembered. Because he is

[2] *Mandate to Witness,* p. 63.

[3] On these two heroes and prophets—and for sheerly rewarding reading—see James Armstrong, *Wilderness Voices* (Nashville: Abingdon Press, 1974).

our Lord, his rebellion gets our attention, alerts our allegiance, and gains our support.

All of the New Testament was written by the primitive church. It is no accident, however, that the post-resurrection epistles use the title "Lord" more often than do the Gospels. Paul and the others clearly saw that if he is not Lord then nothing else that might be affirmed about him—teacher, prophet, what have you—would matter much or last long.

Note, though, where this Lordship was discerned. Jesus tells Mary, in Matthew's account, "Go and tell my brethren" (oh, the tenderness of that: "brethren" despite the failures and desertion), "Go and tell my brethren to go to Galilee, and there they will see me" (28:10). Galilee was back to duty, back to the dust and to the dull dailiness of life, away from the Holy City and its sacred memories, immersed once more in the hubbub and the humdrum, in the hurts and hopes of the ordinary and the everyday.

That indeed is where we do meet him. It is relatively easy to get inspired, sometimes even moved, amidst the pulse of high events: in the hush of a candlelight Communion, in the stately cadences and masterly tones of great music. Moreover, the meeting of him in those places is quite real. It is not, however, quite enough. The Lordship comes, and is owned, as hard decisions are weighed and made, as tender values are toughened and vivified, by being lived out in the arenas of the academy, the metropolis, and the home. Galilee is where he is to be met and recognized—where the sweat is, and the faltering, and the mini-victories.

Some years ago I preached a sermon entitled "When God Said 'Yes.'" It occurs to me now that Easter is also that triumphant time when God said "No." "And the No meant that you didn't have to settle down in grim facts—the cross was the worst of them—or in any of those spotty little anecdotes that seem to make up our life: not in a world where Christmas comes out of a stable, and the Son of God out of a smelly little village, and twenty centuries of Christianity out of a tomb."[4]

And then this. Despite Jesus' question, "Whom are you seeking?" Mary really did not find Jesus. Jesus found Mary.

Mark that well, you weary ones to whom Christ seems far away. We do not find Jesus. Jesus finds us. He makes this forever clear in that miniature version of the gospel so finely chiseled in the fifteenth chapter of Luke: the chapter about the lost coin, the lost lamb, the lost boy. Even the parable of the prodigal, heartening and exquisite though it be, is not the whole gospel. The prodigal came home. He sought, because he could and would. But what about that tiny lamb, wounded and trapped amidst the sharp rocks on the hillside? What about that silver coin, rolled out of sight in some corner of darkness? What could the coin do to get itself found? The answer of course is precisely: nothing.

[4] Paul Scherer, *The Word God Sent* (New York: Harper, 1965), pp. 189-90.

But the Master—he tells us this himself—will keep looking and looking and looking "until he finds it" (15:4). A lamp will be lighted, the sweeping will not stop, a hand will keep feeling in the darkness till the helpless but precious coin is safely in its owner's keep once more.

That's the gospel—not seeking and finding but sought and found:

> It was not I that found, O Savior true;
> No, I was found of thee.

That is what Easter comes down to after all, and above all: that the God of all grace and glory does not wait, like some Oriental potentate, to be sought after and entreated. No! The "Father came out and entreated him" (Luke 15:28b)—that is the gospel of the prodigal love of God. Our God is on the move—onto a Cross and out of a Tomb; into the ghettos and galleries, the senate chambers and hospital rooms; on the move: toward us, for us, in and through us, in the name and for the sake of Jesus Christ our Living Lord.

INDEX